Miriam the Prophetess

Gwen Mouliert

Library of Congress Control Number: 2018945523
ISBN-13:   Paperback: 978-1-64151-871-0

Printed in the United States of America

LitFire
PUBLISHING

LitFire LLC
1-800-511-9787
www.litfirepublishing.com
order@litfirepublishing.com

CONTENTS

Chapter One: Miriam as Protector

Chapter Two: Rhythms of Worship

Chapter Three: Me and My Big mouth

Chapter Four: It is Well With my Soul

CHAPTER ONE

I NEED MY BIG SISTER

Miriam is the first woman in the Old Testament who is given the title prophetess. Deborah and Huldah are also named as prophetess in the Old Testament, along with the wife of Isaiah even through her name is not mentioned the bible tells us that Isaiah's wife was a prophetess. Anna in the New Testament is a prophetess who spoke about Jesus to everyone in the synagogue. The definition of a prophetess is one who speaks from or for God.

However, before Miriam receives this recognition, there are several powerful things spoken about this woman. There are four significant events we will look at in each chapter.

1.   **I Need My Big Sister** (Exodus 2)
2.   **Rhythms of Worship** (Exodus 15)
3.   **Me and My Big Mouth** (Numbers 15)
4.   **It Is Well with My Soul** (Numbers 20)

Let's start with the first time she is mentioned in the Bible and in this story, she is not even named, but from the text we know it is Miriam.

Exodus 2:1-10

¹ And there went a man of the house of Levi, and took to wife a daughter of Levi.

² And the woman conceived, and bare a son: and when she saw him that he was a goodly child, she hid him three months.

³ And when she could no longer hide him, she took for him an ark of bulrushes, and daubed it with slime and with pitch, and put the child therein; and she laid it in the flags by the river's brink.

⁴ And his sister stood afar off, to wit what would be done to him.

⁵ And the daughter of Pharaoh came down to wash herself at the river; and her maidens walked along by the river's side; and when she saw the ark among the flags, she sent her maid to fetch it.

⁶ And when she had opened it, she saw the child: and, behold, the babe wept. And she had compassion on him, and said, this is one of the Hebrews' children.

⁷ Then said his sister to Pharaoh's daughter, "Shall I go and call to thee a nurse of the Hebrew women, that she may nurse the child for thee?"

⁸ And Pharaoh's daughter said to her, "Go." And the maid went and called the child's mother.

⁹ And Pharaoh's daughter said unto her, "Take this child away, and nurse it for me, and I will give thee thy wages." And the woman took the child and nursed it.

¹⁰ And the child grew, and she brought him unto Pharaoh's daughter, and he became her son. And she called his name Moses: and she said, because I drew him out of the water.

For many years the children of God had favor in Egypt because of Joseph and his relationship to the Pharaoh. He saved their nation and was considered a hero. However, after the death of Joseph and the death of the Pharaoh, there arose another leader.

What does Exodus 1:8 tell us about the changes in Egypt?

_____

_____

Exodus 1:8

Then a new king, to whom Joseph meant nothing, came to power in Egypt.

What was Pharaoh's fear about the Hebrew people (Exodus 1:9-10)?

_____

_____

Exodus 1:9-10

⁹ "Look," he said to his people, "the Israelites have become far too numerous for us.

¹⁰ Come, we must deal shrewdly with them or they will become even more numerous and, if war breaks out, will join our enemies, fight against us and leave the country."

Because of the number of Hebrew people in Egypt, Pharaoh made a decree that all the baby boys born were to be killed at birth. It is at this time that the parents of Miriam delivered a male child, of course we know him as Moses (or Charlton Heston/1956). Here is the first time we meet Moses sister Miriam.

Miriam was not afraid to speak up!

Who did Miriam speak to (Exodus 2:7)?

_____

_____

Exodus 2:7

Then his sister asked Pharaoh's daughter, "Shall I go and get one of the Hebrew women to nurse the baby for you?"

What was her suggestion? How does this suggestion benefit her family (Exodus 2:8-9)?

_____

_____

Exodus 2:8-9

[8] "Yes, go," she answered. So, the girl went and got the baby's mother.

[9] Pharaoh's daughter said to her, "Take this baby and nurse him for me, and I will pay you." So, the woman took the baby and nursed him.

Who did she call for (Exodus 2:8)?

_____

_____

Lessons learned from this story!

Can God use us no matter what the situation (Philippians 2:13)?

_____

_____

Philippians 2:13

For it is God who works in you to will and to act in order to fulfill his good purpose.

What do we need from God to speak on the behalf of someone else (Deuteronomy 31:6)?

_____

_____

Deuteronomy 31:6

Be strong and courageous. Do not be afraid or terrified because of them, for the Lord your God goes with you; he will never leave you nor forsake you."

Will God give us wisdom if we ask (James 1:5)?

_____

_____

James 1:5

If any of you lacks wisdom, you should ask God, who gives generously to all without finding fault, and it will be given to you.

In summary, the first time we see Miriam she is watching over her brother, she has the courage to speak up to none other than the Pharaoh's daughter, and she uses wisdom when mentioning finding a nurse for the baby; that was genius.

She was then able to return Moses to his own mother, so she could breastfeed him for many months. What joy must have been in the heart of Jochebed when Miriam came to the house holding her little brother.

Therefore, we know that Miriam was not self-centered, but she cared about someone else's welfare, and extended herself to do what she could to help.

May God give us this ability, also.

As we know, Moses was taken into the home of Pharaoh's daughter and lived in Egypt as a prince for 40 years. Exodus 2 tells us that when Moses was a grown man he saw an Egyptian beating a Hebrew, he went to the defense of his Hebrew brother and ended up killing the Egyptian. Then Moses tried to hide this murder and he hid the dead man's body in the sand. The next day two Hebrew men were fighting and before Moses could intervene they asked, "Do you intend to kill us like you killed the Egyptian yesterday?"

Then Pharaoh heard about what Moses had done and he sought to slay Moses. So, Moses had to run for his life. He ended up in the home of a priest from Midian, he married one of the priest's daughters and spent many years (40 years) as a shepherd.

Moses had three 40 years event cycles: 40 years as a **prince**, 40 years as a **pauper** in the dessert, and 40 years as a **prophet.** For more details on these time periods read the sermon given by Stephen in the book of Acts. Here are the stats to ponder:

How old was Moses when he defended the Hebrew (Acts 7:23)?

_____

_____

Acts 7:23

When Moses was forty years old, he decided to visit his own people, the Israelites.

How long had he been in the desert when God called him (Acts 7:30)?

_____

_____

Acts 7:30

"After forty years had passed, an angel appeared to Moses in the flames of a burning bush in the desert near Mount Sinai.

How long did he wander in the dessert (Acts 7:36)?

_____

_____

Acts 7:36

He led them out of Egypt and performed wonders and signs in Egypt, at the Red Sea and for forty years in the wilderness.

_____

_____

How important is the Number 40? This number is talked about 146 times in the Bible. It represents a time of testing, trial, or probation.

In Exodus 24:18, 34:1-28. Moses received God's law on Mount Sinai during 40 days and nights stay. And through Numbers 13:25; 14:34; 32:13 we learned that the Israelite spies were sent into the promise land for 40 days.

Exodus 24:18

Then Moses entered the cloud as he went on up the mountain. And he stayed on the mountain forty days and forty nights.

Exodus 34:1-28

[1] The Lord said to Moses, "Chisel out two stone tablets like the first ones, and I will write on them the words that were on the first tablets, which you broke.

[2] Be ready in the morning, and then come up on Mount Sinai. Present yourself to me there on top of the mountain.

[3] No one is to come with you or be seen anywhere on the mountain; not even the flocks and herds may graze in front of the mountain."

[4] So Moses chiseled out two stone tablets like the first ones and went up Mount Sinai early in the morning, as the Lord had commanded him; and he carried the two stone tablets in his hands.

[5] Then the Lord came down in the cloud and stood there with him and proclaimed his name, the Lord.

[6] And he passed in front of Moses, proclaiming, "The Lord, the Lord, the compassionate and gracious God, slow to anger, abounding in love and faithfulness,

7 Maintaining love to thousands, and forgiving wickedness, rebellion and sin. Yet he does not leave the guilty unpunished; he punishes the children and their children for the sin of the parents to the third and fourth generation."

8 Moses bowed to the ground at once and worshiped.

9 "Lord," he said, "if I have found favor in your eyes, then let the Lord go with us. Although this is a stiff-necked people, forgive our wickedness and our sin, and take us as your inheritance."

10 Then the Lord said: "I am making a covenant with you. Before all your people I will do wonders never before done in any nation in all the world. The people you live among will see how awesome is the work that I, the Lord, will do for you.

11 Obey what I command you today. I will drive out before you the Amorites, Canaanites, Hittites, Perizzites, Hivites and Jebusites.

12 Be careful not to make a treaty with those who live in the land where you are going, or they will be a snare among you.

13 Break down their altars, smash their sacred stones and cut down their Asherah poles.

14 Do not worship any other god, for the Lord, whose name is Jealous, is a jealous God.

15 Be careful not to make a treaty with those who live in the land; for when they prostitute themselves to their gods and sacrifice to them, they will invite you and you will eat their sacrifices.

¹⁶ And when you choose some of their daughters as wives for your sons and those daughters prostitute themselves to their gods, they will lead your sons to do the same.

¹⁷ Do not make any idols.

¹⁸ Celebrate the Festival of Unleavened Bread. For seven days eat bread made without yeast, as I commanded you. Do this at the appointed time in the month of Aviv, for in that month you came out of Egypt.

¹⁹ The first offspring of every womb belongs to me, including all the firstborn males of your livestock, whether from herd or flock.

²⁰ Redeem the firstborn donkey with a lamb, but if you do not redeem it, break its neck. Redeem all your firstborn sons. No one is to appear before me empty-handed.

²¹ Six days you shall labor, but on the seventh day you shall rest; even during the plowing season and harvest you must rest.

²² Celebrate the Festival of Weeks with the First fruits of the wheat harvest, and the Festival of Ingathering at the turn of the year.

²³ Three times a year all your men are to appear before the Sovereign Lord, the God of Israel.

²⁴ I will drive out nations before you and enlarge your territory, and no one will cover your land when you go up three times each year to appear before the Lord your God.

²⁵ Do not offer the blood of a sacrifice to me along with anything containing yeast, and do not let any of the sacrifice from the Passover Festival remain until morning.

²⁶ Bring the best of the first fruits of your soil to the house of the Lord your God. Do not cook a young goat in its mother's milk."

²⁷ Then the Lord said to Moses, "Write down these words, for in accordance with these words I have made a covenant with you and with Israel."

²⁸ Moses was there with the Lord forty days and forty nights without eating bread or drinking water. And he wrote on the tablets the words of the covenant - the Ten Commandments.

Numbers 13:25

At the end of forty days they returned from exploring the land.

Numbers 14:34

For forty years - one year for each of the forty days you explored the land - you will suffer for your sins and know what it is like to have me against you.'

Numbers 32:13

The Lord's anger burned against Israel and he made them wander in the wilderness forty years, until the whole generation of those who had done evil in his sight was gone.

The prophet Jonah warned Nineveh about their sin for 40 days. (Jonah 3:4)

Jonah 3:4

Jonah began by going a day's journey into the city, proclaiming, "Forty more days and Nineveh will be overthrown."

Ezekiel lay on his right side for 40 days. (Ezekiel 4:6)

Ezekiel 4:6

"After you have finished this, lie down again, this time on your right side, and bear the sin of the people of Judah. I have assigned you 40 days, a day for each year.

Elijah went without food for 40 days at Mount Horeb. (1Kings 19:1-9)

1 Kings 19:1-9 Elijah Flees to Horeb

¹ Now Ahab told Jezebel everything Elijah had done and how he had killed all the prophets with the sword.

² So Jezebel sent a messenger to Elijah to say, "May the gods deal with me, be it ever so severely, if by this time tomorrow I do not make your life like that of one of them."

³ Elijah was afraid and ran for his life. When he came to Beersheba in Judah, he left his servant there,

⁴ While he himself went a day's journey into the wilderness. He came to a broom bush, sat down under it and prayed that he might die. "I have had enough, Lord," he said. "Take my life; I am no better than my ancestors."

⁵ Then he lay down under the bush and fell asleep. All at once an angel touched him and said, "Get up and eat."

⁶ He looked around, and there by his head was some bread baked over hot coals, and a jar of water. He ate and drank and then lay down again.

⁷ The angel of the Lord came back a second time and touched him and said, "Get up and eat, for the journey is too much for you."

⁸ So he got up and ate and drank. Strengthened by that food, he traveled forty days and forty nights until he reached Horeb, the mountain of God.

⁹ There he went into a cave and spent the night.

Satan tried to tempt Jesus many times over 40 days of His fasting. (Matthew 4:1-11)

Matthew 4:1-11

¹ Then Jesus was led by the Spirit into the wilderness to be tempted by the devil.

² After fasting forty days and forty nights, he was hungry.

³ The tempter came to him and said, "If you are the Son of God, tell these stones to become bread."

⁴ Jesus answered, "It is written: 'Man shall not live on bread alone, but on every word that comes from the mouth of God."

⁵ Then the devil took him to the holy city and had him stand on the highest point of the temple.

⁶ "If you are the Son of God," he said, "throw yourself down. For it is written: He will command his angels concerning you and

they will lift you up in their hands, so that you will not strike your foot against a stone."

7 Jesus answered him, "It is also written: 'Do not put the Lord your God to the test.'"

8 Again, the devil took him to a very high mountain and showed him all the kingdoms of the world and their splendor.

9 "All this I will give you," he said, "if you will bow down and worship me."

10 Jesus said to him, "Away from me, Satan! For it is written: 'Worship the Lord your God and serve him only.'"

11 Then the devil left him, and angels came and attended him.

Jesus appeared to others 40 days after His resurrection. (Acts 1:3)

Acts 1:3

After his suffering, he presented himself to them and gave many convincing proofs that he was alive. He appeared to them over a period of forty days and spoke about the kingdom of God.

After reading all these stories and scriptures what speaks to you most about the number 40?

_____

_____

There are more examples, but this is a bible study about Miriam, so I won't go into the details of all the plagues, the Passover, and the deliverance from Egypt. However, please know that for over 400 years these people of God were in captivity.

CHAPTER TWO

RHYTHMS IN WORSHIP

Now God has delivered his people from Egypt and they have passed through the Red Sea, they have witnessed their enemy drowned in the sea, and we now see Miriam in Exodus 15. In the beginning of the chapter Moses begins to sing; it is often called the song of Moses. And it is recorded from Exodus 15:1-18.

Many bibles have caption listed before Exodus 15:19 in the King James Version it says "Miriam's song" she is responding to the song of Moses.

Back in the 1980's we use to sing a song founded on these verses, and it brought great joy to our hearts. We celebrated the victory of the horse and the rider thrown into the Red Sea and we sang it with much gusto. But can we even begin to image the joy that the children of God celebrated that day when they beheld with their own eyes the death and defeat of their greatest enemies?

What title is given to Miriam (Exodus 15:20)?

_____

_____

Exodus 15:1-20 The Song of Moses and Miriam

¹ Then Moses and the Israelites sang this song to the Lord "I will sing to the Lord, for he is highly exalted. Both horse and driver he has hurled into the sea.

² The Lord is my strength and my defense he has become my salvation. He is my God, and I will praise him, my father's God, and I will exalt him.

³ The Lord is a warrior; the Lord is his name.

⁴ Pharaoh's chariots and his army he has hurled into the sea. The best of Pharaoh's officers are drowned in the Red Sea.

⁵ The deep waters have covered them; they sank to the depths like a stone.

⁶ Your right hand, Lord, was majestic in power. Your right hand, Lord, shattered the enemy.

⁷ In the greatness of your majesty you threw down those who opposed you. You unleashed your burning anger; it consumed them like stubble.

⁸ By the blast of your nostrils the waters piled up. The surging waters stood up like a wall; the deep waters congealed in the heart of the sea.

⁹ The enemy boasted, 'I will pursue, I will overtake them. I will divide the spoils; I will gorge myself on them. I will draw my sword and my hand will destroy them.'

¹⁰ But you blew with your breath, and the sea covered them. They sank like lead in the mighty waters.

[11] Who among the gods is like you, Lord? Who is like you - majestic in holiness, awesome in glory, working wonders?

[12] You stretch out your right hand, and the earth swallows your enemies.

[13] In your unfailing love you will lead the people you have redeemed. In your strength you will guide them to your holy dwelling.

[14] The nations will hear and tremble; anguish will grip the people of Philistia.

[15] The chiefs of Edom will be terrified, the leaders of Moab will be seized with trembling, the people of Canaan will melt away;

[16] Terror and dread will fall on them. By the power of your arm they will be as still as a stone - until your people pass by, Lord, until the people you bought pass by.

[17] You will bring them in and plant them on the mountain of your inheritance - the place, Lord, you made for your dwelling, the sanctuary, Lord, your hands established.

[18] The Lord reigns for ever and ever.

[19] When Pharaoh's horses, chariots and horsemen went into the sea, the Lord brought the waters of the sea back over them, but the Israelites walked through the sea on dry ground.

[20] Then Miriam the Prophetess, Aaron's sister, took a timbrel in her hand, and all the women followed her, with timbrels and dancing.

Whose sister was Miriam (Numbers 26:59)?

_____

_____

Numbers 26:59

The name of Amram's wife was Jochebed, a descendant of Levi, who was born to the Levites in Egypt. To Amram she bore Aaron, Moses and their sister Miriam.

What was in her hand (Exodus 15:20)?

_____

_____

What did she do physically to celebrate (Exodus 15:20)?

_____

_____

When they danced whom did they sing about (1Samuel 29:5)?

_____

_____

1 Samuel 29:5

Isn't this the David they sang about in their dances: 'Saul has slain his thousands, and David his tens of thousands'?

What do timbrels or tambourines represent (Jeremiah 31:4)?

_____

_____

Jeremiah 31:4

I will build you up again, and you, Virgin Israel, will be rebuilt.

Again, you will take up your timbrels and go out to dance with the joyful.

The first thing we saw about Miriam is that she was a protector; here we see that she is a prophetess and a worshipper. That she led the women, there is a very strong verse that tells us that she not only led women, but that God used her to help lead the nation.

Who did God set before the people of Israel as leaders (Micah 6:4)?

_____

_____

Micah 6:4

I brought you up out of Egypt and redeemed you from the land of slavery. I sent Moses to lead you, also Aaron and Miriam.

Moses became a great deliverer, Aaron became the first high priest and Miriam is the first prophetess in the Bible.

Lord we thank you that we also have been delivered out of Egypt by one greater than Moses, and now we are a royal priesthood, to offer up praises even as Miriam did. We celebrate our Savior who is worthy of all our praise.

CHAPTER THREE

ME AND MY BIG MOUTH

Miriam is punished

There is a story in Numbers 12 that calls for our attention. Here is a helpful synopsis:

- Miriam and Aaron are jealous of Moses (Numbers 12:1-2)
- Moses was the most humble person on earth (Numbers 12:3)
- God instructed Miriam, Aaron, and Moses to come to the tent of the congregation (Numbers 12:4-5)
- God rebuked Aaron and Miriam for speaking against Moses (Numbers 12:6-9)
- God punished Miriam with leprosy (Numbers 12:10-13)
- Miriam was put outside the camp for 7 days until she was brought back (Numbers 12:14-15)
- The Israelites left Hazeroth and encamped in the Desert of Paran (Numbers 12:16)

Numbers 12:1-16

¹ And Miriam and Aaron spake against Moses because of the Ethiopian woman whom he had married: for he had married an Ethiopian woman.

² And they said, "Hath the LORD indeed spoken only by Moses? Hath he not spoken also by us?" And the LORD heard it.

³ (Now the man Moses was very meek, above all the men which were upon the face of the earth.)

⁴ And the LORD spake suddenly unto Moses, and unto Aaron, and unto Miriam, "Come out ye three unto the tabernacle of the congregation". And they three came out.

⁵ And the LORD came down in the pillar of the cloud, and stood in the door of the tabernacle, and called Aaron and Miriam: and they both came forth.

⁶ And he said, "Hear now my words: If there be a prophet among you, I the LORD will make myself known unto him in a vision, and will speak unto him in a dream.

⁷ My servant Moses is not so, who is faithful in all mine house.

⁸ With him will I speak mouth to mouth, even apparently, and not in dark speeches; and the similitude of the LORD shall he behold: wherefore then were ye not afraid to speak against my servant Moses?"

⁹ And the anger of the LORD was kindled against them; and he departed.

¹⁰ And the cloud departed from off the tabernacle; and, behold, Miriam became leprous, white as snow: and Aaron looked upon Miriam, and, behold, she was leprous.

¹¹ And Aaron said unto Moses," Alas, my lord, I beseech thee, lay not the sin upon us, wherein we have done foolishly, and wherein we have sinned.

¹² Let her not be as one dead, of whom the flesh is half consumed when he cometh out of his mother's womb."

¹³ And Moses cried unto the LORD, saying, "Heal her now, O God, I beseech thee."

¹⁴ And the LORD said unto Moses, "If her father had but spit in her face, should she not be ashamed seven days? let her be shut out from the camp seven days, and after that let her be received in again."

¹⁵ And Miriam was shut out from the camp seven days: and the people journeyed not till Miriam was brought in again.

¹⁶ And afterward the people removed from Hazeroth and pitched in the wilderness of Paran.

Whose name is mentioned first in the opening (Numbers 12:1)?
_____
_____

What do you think the issue is in Numbers 12:2?
_____
_____

When the Lord spoke in Numbers 12:4 how did He call them out?

_____

_____

Who was singled out of the three (Numbers 12:5)?

_____

_____

Why do you think Aaron is listed first when we know from Numbers 12:1 that Miriam was the first name listed?

_____

_____

God was angry that they disrespected Moses and his place of authority; we need to be careful not to speak against God's people, murmuring and complaining never ends well. (1 Chronicles 16:22, Isaiah 54:17)

1 Chronicles 16:22

Saying, Touch not mine anointed, and do my prophets no harm.

Isaiah 54:17

No weapon that is formed against thee shall prosper; and every tongue that shall rise against thee in judgment thou shalt condemn. This is the heritage of the servants of the Lord, and their righteousness is of me, saith the Lord.

Be glad that this bible study is about Miriam and not about speaking against God's servants. Let us see what happens to our sister as a result of the intense punishment.

What did God inflict on Miriam in Numbers 12:10?

Numbers 12:10

And the cloud departed from off the tabernacle; and, behold, Miriam became leprous, white as snow: and Aaron looked upon Miriam, and, behold, she was leprous.

Leprosy was judgment from God that renders a person unclean; there are several people in the Bible that received this chastisement besides Miriam.

What happened to Gehazi the servant of Elisha when he lied (2 Kings 5:20-27)?

---

2 Kings 5:20-27

20 Gehazi, the servant of Elisha the man of God, said to himself, "My master was too easy on Naaman, this Aramean, by not accepting from him what he brought. As surely as the Lord lives, I will run after him and get something from him."

21 So Gehazi hurried after Naaman. When Naaman saw him running toward him, he got down from the chariot to meet him. "Is everything all right?" he asked.

22 "Everything is all right," Gehazi answered. "My master sent me to say, 'Two young men from the company of the prophets have just come to me from the hill country of Ephraim. Please give them a talent[a] of silver and two sets of clothing.'"

23 "By all means, take two talents," said Naaman. He urged Gehazi to accept them, and then tied up the two talents of silver in two bags, with two sets of clothing. He gave them to two of his servants, and they carried them ahead of Gehazi.

24 When Gehazi came to the hill, he took the things from the servants and put them away in the house. He sent the men away and they left.

25 When he went in and stood before his master, Elisha asked him, "Where have you been, Gehazi?" "Your servant didn't go anywhere," Gehazi answered.

26 But Elisha said to him, "Was not my spirit with you when the man got down from his chariot to meet you? Is this the time to take money or to accept clothes - or olive groves and vineyards, or flocks and herds, or male and female slaves?

27 Naaman's leprosy will cling to you and to your descendants forever." Then Gehazi went from Elisha's presence and his skin was leprous - it had become as white as snow.

And another profound story –

What happened to King Uzziah because of his pride (2 Chronicles 26:21)?

_____

_____

2 Chronicles 26:21

King Uzziah had leprosy until the day he died. He lived in a separate house - leprous and banned from the temple of the Lord. Jotham his son had charge of the palace and governed the people of the land.

Each of these stories tell us that this leprosy was from the Lord first as a punishment, Miriam was smitten because she murmured, Gehazi was smitten because he coveted and lied. Uzziah was a leper because of his pride. I have been guilty of these same sins.

We have a tendency to blame everything on the devil but there are times because of our actions and the choices we make, that we are considered spiritual lepers. But be of good cheer, Jesus heals leprosy.

What does Jesus do to heal the leper (Matthew 8:3)?

_____

_____

Matthew 8:3

Jesus reached out his hand and touched the man. "I am willing," he said. "Be clean!" Immediately he was cleansed of his leprosy.

What was the condition of the leper after Jesus spoke (Mark1:42)?

_____

_____

Mark 1:42

Immediately the leprosy left him, and he was cleansed.

Do you think that this leper had faith in his healer (Luke 5:12-13)? Why? Or, why not?

_____

_____

_____

_____

Luke 5:12-13

¹² While Jesus was in one of the towns, a man came along who was covered with leprosy. When he saw Jesus, he fell with his face to the ground and begged him, "Lord, if you are willing, you can make me clean."

¹³ Jesus reached out his hand and touched the man. "I am willing," he said. "Be clean!" And immediately the leprosy left him.

How was Miriam's leprosy healed (Numbers 12:13)?

_____

_____

Numbers 12:13

So Moses cried out to the Lord, "Please, God, Heal her!"

Before Moses prayed for Miriam's healing, Miriam and her brother Aaron had to repent (Numbers 12:11).

Numbers 12:11

And Aaron said unto Moses, Alas, my lord, I beseech thee, *lay not the sin upon **us,** wherein **we** have done foolishly, and wherein **we** have sinned.*

So, they both sinned, but Aaron did not receive the same punishment as his sister. I pondered this for a long time, because it did not seem fair to punish Miriam only. They both sinned, but it seems that only Miriam was held accountable.

I want to share something that may help us understand this situation. In the book of Leviticus no one with leprosy could serve God, and since Aaron was going to become a high priest, if he ever had leprosy he would have been disqualified from his service and would have never become a priest.

Leviticus 13 is the law of the leper: It is a long chapter, Leviticus 13:59 tells about being unclean and all of its restrictions.

Leviticus 13:59

These are the regulations concerning defiling molds in woolen or linen clothing, woven or knitted material, or any leather article, for pronouncing them clean or unclean.

Leviticus 13:45-46 sums this up for us.

Leviticus 13:45-46

[45] And the leper in whom the plague is, his clothes shall be rent, and his head bare, and he shall put a covering upon his upper lip, and shall cry, Unclean, unclean.

[46] All the days wherein the plague shall be in him he shall be defiled; he is unclean: he shall dwell alone; without the camp shall his habitation be.

God even gave Aaron specific instructions about this; there were so many things that could disqualify him from his service to God.

Leviticus 21:17-24

[17] Speak unto Aaron, saying, "Whosoever he be of thy seed in their generations that hath any blemish, let him not approach to offer the bread of his God.

¹⁸ For whatsoever man he be that hath a blemish, he shall not approach: a blind man, or a lame, or he that hath a flat nose, or anything superfluous,

¹⁹ Or a man that is broken footed, or brokenhanded,

²⁰ Or crookback, or a dwarf, or that hath a blemish in his eye, or be scurvy, or scabbed, or hath his stones broken;

²¹ No man that hath a blemish of the seed of Aaron the priest shall come nigh to offer the offerings of the Lord made by fire: he hath a blemish; he shall not come nigh to offer the bread of his God.

²² He shall eat the bread of his God, both of the most holy, and of the holy.

²³ Only he shall not go in unto the veil, nor come nigh unto the altar, because he hath a blemish; that he profane not my sanctuaries: for I the Lord do sanctify them."

²⁴ And Moses told it unto Aaron, and to his sons, and unto all the children of Israel.

So many of us have blemishes and at times feel unclean, please don't let this keep you from the presence of God.

Why do we need to be cleansed from sin (Psalm 51:2)?

_____

_____

Psalm 51:2

Wash away all my iniquity and cleanse me from my sin.

What is hyssop (Psalm 51:7)?

_____

_____

Psalm 51:7

Cleanse me with hyssop, and I will be clean; wash me, and I will be whiter than snow.

Hyssop was a branch from a small bush and the first time we find it in the Word of God it was used in the greatest of ways. On the night of the first Passover they were told to kill a lamb and that they were to sprinkle the blood of the lamb on their door posts for protection for all that were inside.

Exodus 12:22

And ye shall take a bunch of hyssop, and dip it in the blood that is in the basin and strike the lintel and the two side posts with the blood that is in the basin; and none of you shall go out at the door of his house until the morning.

The blood on the Hyssop bush was in connection with the blood of an innocent lamb. The last time we see hyssop it once again represents the blood of the Lamb.

John 19:28-30

28 After this, Jesus knowing that all things were now accomplished, that the scripture might be fulfilled, saith, I thirst.

29 Now there was set a vessel full of vinegar: and they filled a sponge with vinegar, and put it upon hyssop, and put it to his mouth.

³⁰ When Jesus therefore had received the vinegar, he said, "It is finished." and he bowed his head and gave up the ghost.

When Jesus was on the cross and he said I thirst and they brought him vinegar and when it was put to his lips He said "it is finished" notice that the item used to give him the vinegar was Hyssop. So, the first time and the last time we see hyssop in the bible it represents that blood of the Lamb and that is what cleanses us from all sin.

Psalm 51:10

Create in me a pure heart, O God, and renew a steadfast spirit within me.

2 Corinthians 5:17

Therefore, if anyone is in Christ, the **new** creation has come: The old has gone, the **new** is here!

Colossians 3:10

And have put on the new self, which is being renewed in knowledge in the image of its Creator.

God chooses to forget our sins, how does that make you feel? (Jeremiah 33:8; Jeremiah 31:34)

_____

_____

Jeremiah 33:8

I will cleanse them from all the sin they have committed against me and will forgive all their sins of rebellion against me.

Jeremiah 31:34

"They will not teach again, each man his neighbor and each man his brother, saying, 'Know the LORD,' for they will all know Me, from the least of them to the greatest of them," declares the LORD, "for I will forgive their iniquity, and their sin I will remember no more."

God forgives and forgets, we need to do the same so we can walk in His mercy, grace and forgiveness. He still used Miriam in a powerful way once she was forgiven and cleansed.

Describe the areas of God's mercy in your life. (Titus 3:5)?

_____

_____

_____

_____

Titus 3:5

He saved us, not because of righteous things we had done, but because of his mercy. He saved us through the washing of rebirth and renewal by the Holy Spirit,

If we confess our sins – God's pardon is always equated with confession, and there is no promise of pardon unless a full acknowledgment has been made.

When was the last time that you confessed your sins to God (1 John 1:9)?

_____

_____

_____

_____

1 John 1:9

If we confess our sins, he is faithful and just and will forgive us our sins and purify us from all unrighteousness.

When we praise the Lord for his cleansing and forgiveness does that help you to enter into His presence? If so, how?

_____

_____

Lord, please keep us aware of jealousy and any disrespect to our leaders, that might try and creep into our lives. We don't want to be unclean and allow anything to separate us from you. Thank you for cleansing us from all spiritual leprosy.

Even as Moses prayed for his sister, give us a burden to pray for one another. And thank you again for unconditional love and forgiveness.

CHAPTER FOUR

IT IS WELL WITH MY SOUL

After the story found in Numbers 12 we do not read much written about Miriam. She is mentioned in Numbers 26:59, which gives us the birth order of the children of Jochebed, and again in Deuteronomy 24:9 when the children of Israel are told to remember what happened to Miriam and her punishment.

Numbers 26:59

And the name of Amram's wife was Jochebed, the daughter of Levi, whom her mother bore to Levi in Egypt: and she bore to Amram Aaron and Moses, and Miriam their sister.

Deuteronomy 24:9

Remember what the Lord your God did to Miriam on the way as you came out of Egypt.

We need to remember that she repented, she was cleansed and forgiven, let us not forget the godliness of her brother Moses who prayed for her after she came against him.

They were in the desert of Zin; the definition of Zin is thorn. All of us have challenges in life and there have been thorns since the fall in the garden. The Bible says that Miriam was buried in Kadesh and not in Zin (Numbers 20:1).

Numbers 20:1

Then came the children of Israel, even the whole congregation, into the desert of Zin in the first month: and the people abode in Kadesh; and Miriam died there and was buried there.

Kadesh means holy, consecrated, sanctified, set apart for a purpose. As we end this lesson on Miriam, she was set apart for a purpose.

Miriam's cup (Kos Miryam) is used as a symbolic item at the Seder table at Passover. This cup is filled with water to represent that a well of water followed Miriam with the Israelites as they wandered for forty years in the wilderness. There was no water after her death until Moses and Aaron sought God for provision. The cup honors Miriam for her support and nurturing of her family (Telushkin, 1997 & Ginzberg, 2017).

The first purpose that we saw concerning Miriam was that she was a **protection** of her family.

Her second purpose is that she becomes a **praiser of** the Lord for all the great deliverances He has given us.

The third purpose was to be a **prophetess** for the Lord.

The fourth purpose is to understand **pardon.**

The fifth event in her life was to be buried in Kadesh: place of consecration to the Lord. She was **pure** before the Lord.

May each of us learn from these valuable lessons from the life of Miriam the first women prophetess.

Lord please help us to love and protect our families and loved ones as she did. That each of us can speak for the Lord, and that praise is essential as we love and serve you. That pardon is a prayer away and we desire to live pure lives to your honor and glory. In Jesus name Amen

Interesting that we don't have any recorded written prophecies from Miriam the prophetess yet we can learn valuable lessons from her example.

Activities

1. *Can you think of a time when you were able to protect a family member or defend someone close to you? How did God help you to accomplish this?*

   _____

   _____

   _____

   _____

2. *Try to remember the last time that your family experienced a crisis. What steps were taken to deal with this situation? List those steps that were taken. How did the Lord answer your cry at this time of need?*

   _____

   _____

   _____

   _____

3. *Think about a time when you had an argument with someone. You acted harshly. At that time, you knew that you were right; but later you realized that you were very wrong.*

After this revelation what were your next steps taken to resolve the situation?

_____

_____

Did you repent?

_____

_____

Were you able to go to the person and resolve the problem?

_____

_____

How did God help you change your behavior?

_____

_____

What part did forgiveness play in this event?

_____

_____

4. *Pastors, elders, deacons (1 Timothy 3), husbands (Ephesians 5:22; Colossians 3:18), parents (Ephesians 6:1), bosses (Ephesians 6:5-8) and other leaders (Matthew 8:9) are given authority. We honor them by coming under their authority. To do otherwise is disrespectful and rebellious.*

How good are you at coming under the leader's authority?

_____

_____

How do you handle those times when you realize that you are rebellious or jealous?

_____

_____

What steps do you take to correct the situation? Write down the steps and think on them.

_____

_____

Have you taken the correct direction?

_____

_____

THE HORSE AND RIDER SONG

I will sing unto the Lord for He has triumphed gloriously
The horse and rider thrown into the sea
I will sing unto the Lord for He has triumphed gloriously
The horse and rider thrown into the sea

The Lord, my God, my strength my song
Has now become my victory
The Lord, my God, my strength my song
Has Now Become My Victory

The Lord is God and I will praise Him
My fathers God and I will E-x-a-l-t Him
The Lord is God and I will praise Him
My Fathers God and I will Exalt Him!

(Based on Praise Scriptures from the Bible Exodus 15:1-21)

REFERENCES

Ginzberg, Louis. "Legends of the Jews- Volume 3" Kindle Edition.

New International Version (NIV) Holy Bible, New International Version®, NIV® Copyright ©1973, 1978, 1984, 2011

New King James Version 2000 (NKJ) Copyright ©2000

Telushkin, Joseph. "Biblical Literacy: The Most Important People, Events, and Ideas of the Hebrew Bible." William Morrow: New York, 1997.

Other written materials from Gwen Mouliert.

Satan Secret Weapon:

Now that Jesus is Lord of our lives, we don't practice sin, so the enemy does not have an open door, but he is surd and deceitful and will look for any opportunity to hinder our walk.

Hidden bitterness is one of his greatest weapons, this book exposes his tactics and gives us a plan to attack that really works.

Hyper to Holy:

This book is about how Gwen was saved and filled with the spirit. It is written with great truth and humor, all ages have enjoyed this delightful testimony.

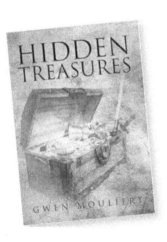

Hidden Treasures:

Over 40 years as a bible teacher, Gwen has been directed by the Lord, to share the 10 most helpful and powerful truths that we can apply to our lives. How to identify a thorn in the flesh, how prophesy to the four winds in times of dryness. Teaching on healing and hearing the voice of God.

If you are interested in Gwen Mouliert's CDs and bible teachings please call our office for a list of items that are available.
609-407-1753 or visit us at www.gwenmouliert.org.

NOTES

Printed in the USA
CPSIA information can be obtained
at www.ICGtesting.com
JSHW020741050923
47608JS00007B/91

9 781641 518710